Permission to quote in critical reviews with citation:
Being a Blue Angel
By Mark I. & Amy C. Sutherland

ISBN 978-0-9832363-9-9

Photo credits: Mark I. Sutherland, Amy C. Sutherland, JC Chandler, U.S. Navy and U.S. Air Force. All photos used with permission.

DUNROBIN PUBLISHING

www.dunrobin.us

To Eili, Keegan, Gavin & Liam

With profound gratitude to:
CDR Garrett Kasper, USN
LT CJ Simonsen, USN
LT Katie Kelly, USN
MC2 Rachel McNabb, USN
LCDR Todd Royles, USN
LT Dave Tickle, USN
Capt Edward Jorge, USMC
CWo4 Clive Dixon, USN
PR1 Rodollo Noriega
AO1 Vincent Dunhill-Cooper
PO1 Dustin Ewing
AM1 Vincent Stolp
AM1 Matthew Bellin
PO2 Fabian Serrano
CMC Yoshimi Core
AT2 William Channing Martin
YN1 Jennifer Jones
HM1 Jonathan Mocer
YN Chanel Campbell
AT1 Curt Metzger
AD2 Zackary Gruwell
GySgt Joe Alley, USMC
Sgt JC Chandler, USMC

The Officers and Crew of the Blue Angels

And All Who Serve!

The Blue Angels

Performing Since 1946

Being A Blue Angel

The U.S. Navy and Marines only take the best, and the Blue Angels are the best of the best.

There are many different jobs you can do as a Blue Angel. You could be a pilot, you could make airshows happen, you could be a doctor, or you could even take photographs, fix the jets or order the parts.

There are 16 officers and nearly 110 Sailors and Marines in the Blue Angels.

They are on the team for 2 or 3 years and then they go back to the Navy or the Marines.

MESSAGE FROM A BLUE
Command Master Chief Yoshimi Core

"Do good in school, study hard, work hard, hang out with good people and don't do drugs!"

CMC Core was born in Japan.
His dad was in the U.S. Air Force.
He worked for the Tampa Bay Buccaneers football team before he joined the Navy!

All Blue Angels are either in the Navy or the Marines. They have to be very good at their job.

To be a Blue, you have to work hard, be honest, and do things right, even when no one else is around. You should also study hard, learn lots of math and science, learn how to write well, play sports, and definitely stay out of trouble.

Maybe you will be a Blue Angel when you are older.

F/A-18 Pilots

A Blue Angel jet is a Boeing F/A-18. Any Navy or Marine F/A-18 pilot can do what the Blue Angel pilots do. But the Blue Angels fly much closer to each other than other F/A-18 pilots. To volunteer to be a Blue Angel jet pilot, you first have to fly an F/A-18 for 1,250 hours during your time in the Navy or the Marines.

Most Blue Angel F/A-18 pilots have also landed on an aircraft carrier more than 250 times before they become a Blue Angel.

Every new Blue Angel pilot is chosen by the other Blue Angel pilots.

During some formations the Blue Angels are only

An F/A-18 can fly at 1,400 miles per hour and could fly all the way across the US in less than 2 hours, if it had enough gas!

4

Everyone who has been a Blue Angel, will always be a Blue Angel.

18 inches apart! That's really, really close!!

10 11 12 13 14 15 16 17 18

Visit
www.BlueAngelsBook.us
to see the
Blue Angels
fly!

After you are done being a Blue Angel pilot you go back to the Navy or the Marines and fly missions off an aircraft carrier again.

MESSAGE FROM A BLUE
LT CJ Simonsen

"Follow your dreams, work hard in school and stay out of trouble. Focus on school early, because that's going to open up many doors, down the road, throughout your life."

LT Simonsen is from Coon Rapids, Minnesota.
He loved math and science as a kid.

Fat Albert Airlines

Fat Albert is a Marine-run Lockheed Martin C-130 transport aircraft. Fat Albert flies all the Blue Angel support staff and all the equipment to the shows. The support staff do everything on the ground during the airshow. Fat Albert also performs in the show.

Fat Albert can carry 30,000 pounds of cargo, plus the Blue Angel team. That's the same as 600 middle schoolers all stacked up.

Fat Albert's engines are more powerful than all the cars in a NASCAR race. Combined!

MESSAGE FROM A BLUE
Captain Edward Jorge

"If you want to be a Blue Angel, you have to set a goal. You should listen to your mom and dad, and your teachers. You should play sports, stay in school and graduate. Follow the rules, and eat your vegetables because vegetables make you strong."

Captain Jorge is from Miami, Florida.

Did You Know?
Every person who works on, or in, Fat Albert is a U.S. Marine!

Fat Albert is as long as two school buses.

Its wingspan is the same as three school buses in a line.

MESSAGE FROM A BLUE
GySgt Joe Alley

"Being a Blue Angel is possible, but it will take a lot of hard work! But don't lose the enthusiasm you have for wanting to be a Blue Angel. If you want to do this job, you can!"

GySgt Alley grew up on a farm in Indiana. He loved to fish!

#7 Jet

Yes! There are 7 Blue Angel jets! The pilot of the #7 jet is the person you hear over the loud speakers during the airshow, telling you what the Blue Angels are doing.

He has to remember what happens next and when to say what is happening, without looking.

#7 gets to the airshow a day before the rest of the team. He makes sure everything the team needs is ready before the rest of the team arrives. He also flies special guests and reporters in his jet before the airshow.

MESSAGE FROM A BLUE
LT Dave Tickle

"You can't be a Blue Angel without good grades and a great education, so study hard! Set goals and work hard to achieve them."

LT Tickle grew up in Birmingham, Alabama. He loved to ride dirt bikes, camp, hike and scuba dive.

Did You Know? #7 is the only Blue Angel jet with 2 seats. On show days it is the spare jet.

How Long Are You A Blue Angel Pilot?

7>6>5

Some pilots join the Blue Angels as the pilot of the #7 jet. The next year they fly #6, and then move to #5 for their final year.

3>4

Other pilots join for only two years and fly the #3 jet and then fly the #4 jet during year two.

1 or 2

And other pilots join as #1 or #2. They are also on the team for only two years.

M3 M2 M1

The Marine pilots of Fat Albert are in the Blue Angels for 3 years.

Visit www.BlueAngelsBook.us to see the author of this book go for a ride in the #7 jet.

How Do Planes Fly?

Airplanes move through the air so fast it's like they are swimming through the sky. A Blue Angel jet can fly at 1,400 miles per hour and could fly from New York to Los Angeles in less than 2 hours. A car would take 2 days if it didn't stop.

When a plane is flying, the air moves under the wings and allows the pilot to make the airplane go up and down, and left and right, using flaps on the wings and tail. But it's important to keep going fast. If the airplane goes too slow, the air stops moving under the wings and the plane will fall out of the sky.

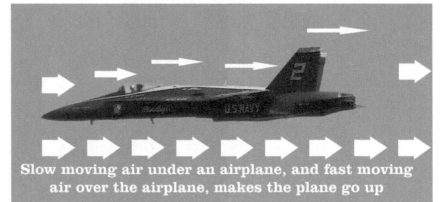

Slow moving air under an airplane, and fast moving air over the airplane, makes the plane go up

And when an airplane turns really fast, the people in the plane feel G-force. See the author fly in the Blue Angel jet and experience Gs at www.BlueAngelsBook.us.

What Is A G?

When airplanes turn really fast they experience G-force or Gs. A G means gravity. Gravity keeps you on the ground. When you are standing still you weigh 1 G. If you were in space, you would weigh 0 Gs. When Gs go up, you weigh more, and your blood wants to go to your feet.

When Fat Albert takes off, the people in the plane feel 2 Gs, or two times normal gravity.

If you normally weigh 50 pounds, at 2 Gs you weigh 100 pounds. During some turns, the F/A-18s are at 7 1/2 Gs. If you normally weighed 50 pounds, you would weigh 475 pounds. The pilots have to be very fit. Using their muscles and breathing, the pilots are able to keep the blood in their heads. Keeping the blood in your head is very important. If a pilot didn't, he would fall asleep in 3 seconds.

Officers

These officers tell everyone what to do. The President of the United States tells them what to do.

Navy Ranks   ## Marine Ranks

When someone is promoted they move to a new rank this way >>>

When you join as an officer you start here or here.

	Navy Ranks	Marine Ranks
O-12 Special	Admiral of the Navy (AN)	
O-11 Special	Fleet Admiral (FADM)	
O-10	Admiral Chief of Naval Operations/ Commandant of the Coast Guard (ADM)	General (Gen)
O-9	Vice Admiral (VADM)	Lieutenant General (LtGen)
O-8	Rear Admiral, Upper Half (RADM)	Major General (MajGen)
O-7	Rear Admiral, Lower Half (RDML)	Brigadier General (BGen)
O-6	Captain (CAPT)	Colonel (Col)
O-5	Commander (CDR)	Lieutenant Colonel (LtCol)
O-4	Lieutenant Commander (LCDR)	Major (Maj)
O-3	Lieutenant (LT)	Captain (Capt)
O-2	Lieutenant Junior Grade (LTJG)	First Lieutenant (1stLt)
O-1	Ensign (ENS)	Second Lieutenant (2ndLt)
W-5	Chief Warrant Officer 5 (CWO5)	Chief Warrant Officer 5 (W5)
W-4	Chief Warrant Officer 4 (CWO4)	Chief Warrant Officer 4 (W4)
W-3	Chief Warrant Officer 3 (CWO3)	Chief Warrant Officer 3 (W3)
W-2	Chief Warrant Officer 2 (CWO2)	Chief Warrant Officer 2 (W2)
W-1	Warrant Officer 1 (WO1)	Warrant Officer 1 (W1)

Different people have different ranks in the military. You can have an officer rank or an enlisted rank. The officers at the top of the page get to tell everyone below them what to do. The officers at the bottom of the page only get to tell the enlisted people what to do.

Enlisteds

People who enlist start at the bottom of this page. They can move up, or train to become an officer.

Navy Ranks   ## Marine Ranks

Pay Grade	Navy Rank	Marine Rank
E-9 Special	Master Chief Petty Officer of the Navy (MCPON)	Sergeant Major of the Marine Corps (SgtMajMarCor)
E-9	Fleet/Command Master Chief Petty Officer (MCPO)	Sergeant Major (SgtMaj)
E-9	Master Chief Petty Officer (MCPO)	Master Gunnery Sergeant (MGySgt)
E-8		First Sergeant (1stSgt)
E-8	Senior Chief Petty Officer (SCPO)	Master Sergeant (MSgt)
E-7	Chief Petty Officer (CPO)	Gunnery Sergeant (GySgt)
E-6	Petty Officer First Class (PO1)	Staff Sergeant (SSgt)
E-5	Petty Officer Second Class (PO2)	Sergeant (Sgt)
E-4	Petty Officer Third Class (PO3)	Corporal (Cpl)
E-3	Seaman (SN)	Lance Cororal (LCpl)
E-2	Seaman Apprentice (SA)	Private First Class (PFC)
E-1	Seaman Recruit (SR)	Private (Pvt)

The enlisted ranks at the top of the page get to tell all the other enlisted men and women what to do. But they all have to do what the officers tell them to do. The enlisted ranks at the bottom of the page have to do what all the officers and enlisteds above them tell them to do.

A Week in the Life

Each winter, the Blue Angels practice 3 times a day, 6 days a week, for 10 weeks, in El Centro, California. Then they perform in airshows all over the country for 8 months.

During the airshow months, they work 6 days a week.

On Tuesday, they practice at Naval Air Station Pensacola in Florida.

On Wednesday, they practice again and sign autographs. #7 and his crew chief fly to the next show. When they land, they make sure everything is ready. They also fly some very lucky guests in the #7 jet.

MESSAGE FROM A BLUE
LCDR Todd Royles

"I got to watch the Blue Angels as a kid and I thought to myself 'one day, I'm going to do that.' Don't ever let anyone set your limits for you."

LCDR Royles is from Willow Grove, Pennsylvania. When he was a kid, he played football and hockey. In the Navy, he graduated from Top Gun!

On Thursday, Fat Albert flies to the show with 45 other Blue Angels on the plane. The six other Blue Angel jets fly from Florida to the airshow. When everyone gets there, they practice again.

On Friday, the Blue Angels visit schools and hospitals to talk to people about the Blue Angels. Then the pilots practice again, usually for an audience of special needs guests.

On Saturday and Sunday, the Blue Angels perform in front of thousands of guests at the airshow. Then they load Fat Albert and everyone flies back to Pensacola in the Blue Angel planes.

On Monday, the Blue Angels take the day off to spend time with family and friends, and get ready for another busy week.

Events Coordination

The Events Team is led by #8, who flies in the backseat of the #7 jet. The Events Team makes sure all the shows are organized according to the Blue Angel support manual. This includes hotels, cars, fuel, permission to fly and much more.

#8 visits all the show sites during the winter with #7. After they visit, the team plans all the Blue Angel shows. To be #8, you first have to be a Navy Flight Officer in the Navy. A Navy Flight Officer flies in the backseat of a fighter jet and is in charge of where to go and the weapons.

MESSAGE FROM A BLUE
YN1 Jennifer Jones

"You can be a Blue Angel one day! Don't give up on your dream!"

YN1 Jones grew up in La Grange, Georgia.

Crew Chiefs

The Crew Chiefs start working at 5 in the morning. They start the engines of the planes and make sure they are ready for the airshows.

The pilot trusts his or her Crew Chief so much that when the pilot is ready to fly the pilot just jumps in the jet and takes off.

MESSAGE FROM A BLUE
AT2 William Channing Martin

"Set some goals, stay in school and don't do drugs. Anything you want to do is possible. When I was 8, I saw my first Blue Angel show and I thought it was the coolest thing in the world. And now, I'm a Blue Angel. It's a dream come true!"

AT2 Martin grew up in Belmont, Massachusetts. He was the oldest of 7 kids! He loved to play basketball and baseball when he was a kid.

Medical

There are two people who are doctors with the Blue Angels. Doc, who is an officer, and Baby Doc, who is an enlisted. You can see more info about officers and enlisteds on pages 12-13.

The doctors keep the other Blue Angels healthy and make sure they feel good enough to do their jobs.

Baby Doc also drives the Blue Angel pilots around during the airshows and takes lots of photographs.

MESSAGE FROM A BLUE
HM1 Jonathan Mocek

"Work hard. Stay in school. And don't let anyone tell you that you can't be what you dream of being."

HM1 Mocek was born in Pennsylvania and grew up in Georgia. When he was a kid he was in marching band, and enjoyed working on cars and houses.

MESSAGE FROM A BLUE
Yeoman Chanel Campbell

"Once a Blue Angel, always a Blue Angel.
If this is what you want to do, then keep going after it."

Yeoman Campbell grew up
in New Orleans, Louisiana.

The Administration Team has an officer, a senior chief and two yeomen. Yeomen are like administrative assistants in an office.

The team is responsible for lots of writing about orders, awards, fitness evaluations, instructions, and anything else the Blue Angels need written down. They handle the mail, vacation requests, legal records, and many other important things.

Each week, they take care of orders and paychecks for the more than 70 Blue Angels who travel to each airshow.

Maintenance Control

The Maintenance Control Team starts work at 5:15 in the morning.

There are thousands of parts on an F/A-18 and on Fat Albert. This team's job is to make sure all of the parts are working, so the planes are ready to fly. If something is broken, they make sure it gets fixed.

Maintenance Control team members have to be good at math and science.

MESSAGE FROM A BLUE
Master Chief Virgil Craven

"School is very important. You have to be smart and the easiest way to get smart is to pay attention in school. Listen to your parents. Take their advice and do the best job you can do in everything you do."

Master Chief Craven grew up in Albany, Missouri, and Lakewood, Washington. When he was a kid, he was in the Boy Scouts, and loved bowling and basketball.

MESSAGE FROM A BLUE
LT Katie Kelly

"Anything is possible, if you put your mind to it. Do well in school. Find sports you enjoy doing. Be a leader!"

LT Kelly grew up in Elgin, Illinois.
When she was a kid, she enjoyed competitive figure skating and swimming. She wanted to be an astronaut.

The Public Affairs Team talks to TV, radio and newspaper reporters about the Blue Angels.

They also take all the photos and videos of the Blue Angels and put them on the web. You can see their work on the Blue Angels' website, Facebook, Twitter and YouTube.

The team also helps authors who write books about the Blue Angels, like this book.

Video

The Video Team is the ground control unit during the airshow. If something goes wrong with a plane during the show, they talk to the pilots and then tell the Maintenance Team what to do to fix the problem.

The team also records video of every practice and airshow. The pilots watch the videos. This helps them fly better.

The team members come from Navy and Marine teams that fix airplanes. When they join the Blue Angels they are trained on how to work in ground control and how to record video.

MESSAGE FROM A BLUE
AT1 Curt Metzger

"Stay in school, stay out of trouble, and work as hard as you can."

AT1 Metzger grew up in St. Petersburg, Florida. He loved to play sports when he was a kid.

It takes a lot of supplies and money to run the Blue Angels. So a Supply Officer makes sure all the money is spent correctly, and a crew of enlisted people help the Supply Officer.

The Supply Team makes sure the Blue Angels have spare parts for the planes and everything else all of the Blue Angels need, like pens, paper, uniforms and jet fuel.

Working together, the Supply Team and the Fat Albert crew can transport a new jet engine to an airshow in 4-6 hours.

MESSAGE FROM A BLUE
Chief Warrant Officer Clive Dixon

"There are many directions you could go. Always ask your parents and other adults how they have done things."

CWO Dixon was born in Jamaica, and grew up in New York City.

MESSAGE FROM A BLUE
PR1 Rodollo Norriega

"Stay in school, do good in school. and listen to your teachers because they can teach you a lot."

PR1 Norriega is from Brownsville, Texas. When he was younger, he was in the Civil Air Patrol.

The Life Support Team works on the jets' ejection seats which rocket a pilot out of the plane if it is going to crash. They also work on the jets' air conditioning and each pilot's flight gear. This team starts working at 4:45 in the morning.

Did You Know? During an ejection, a pilot experiences 14-16 Gs and his or her parachute opens in 1.5 seconds. You can learn more about Gs on page 11.

Power Plants

The Power Plants Team works on the engines and the backup power. They are also in charge of the smoke you see coming from the jets, which is an environmentally-friendly smoke.

The F/A-18's engines can produce 16,000 pounds of thrust. That's a lot of power to push the plane forward, giving the jet a top speed of 1,400 miles per hour. A Blue Angel jet could travel from St. Louis to Chicago in 13 minutes. It would take you five hours to drive.

Each engine costs about $1.5 million, and there are two on each jet!

MESSAGE FROM A BLUE
AD2 Zackary Gruwell

"If you can turn a wrench on a car, you can turn a wrench on one of these jets. Work hard, get good grades, and join the military."

AD2 Gruwell grew up on a Wyoming cattle ranch as a cowboy. He loved to play sports when he was a kid.

Avionics

The Avionics Team takes care of the navigation systems, that help the pilots know where they are and where they need to go, and all the other electronics on the planes like radios and radar. Radar lets the pilots see the ground or other aircraft that are a long way away, day or night.

Part of the team follows the jets before takeoff to make sure they are safe. This team's nickname is "Mobile" because they are just like a mobile NASCAR pit crew. If something is wrong with a jet, the team can get the pilot into a new jet in 5-10 minutes.

MESSAGE FROM A BLUE
Petty Officer First Class Dustin Ewing

"You can't do this unless you finish school. So stay in school, stay out of trouble, and keep your nose clean."

Petty Officer Ewing grew up in Michigan.

MESSAGE FROM A BLUE
AM1 Vincent Stolp

"Teamwork, goals and safety
are important."

AM1 Stolp grew up in Jacksonville, Florida.

The Airframe Team works on the F/A-18s and Fat Albert. They work on the parts of the planes used for landing and controlling the plane when it flies, the hydraulic system that keeps parts oiled so they move, and the structure of the plane, and keep them in good shape.

They also work on the parts that allow the F/A-18s to land and take off on an aircraft carrier.

Paint Shop

The Paint Shop Team makes sure the airplanes stay clean and don't get rusty. They also paint the airplanes and put the decals and numbers on the planes.

If a jet breaks down, they will put a new number on the #7 jet. The team can put a new number on a jet in 10-15 minutes, and then the #7 jet looks just like the #1-#6 jet it is replacing. And the show can go on.

MESSAGE FROM A BLUE
Petty Officer Second Class Fabian Serrano

"If you want to be a Blue Angel, find out through adults what are the steps you need to take. Make yourself a goal, make yourself a plan, and just follow it through. Persistency, motivation, and dedication will get you to whatever you want to be."

Petty Officer Serrano grew up in New York State.

28

Quality Assurance

The Quality Assurance Team, or QA Team, makes sure all the people working on the airplanes do a good job. They make sure everything is safe on the airplanes.

Blue Angels in Quality Assurance are chosen to be in QA after they join the Blue Angels as part of the Maintenance Team.

Senior team members in maintenance, especially those who pay the best attention to detail, are chosen to be in QA.

MESSAGE FROM A BLUE
AO1 Vincent Dunhill-Cooper

"Get your education. Education is the most important part of anything in life, but especially if you want to be a Blue Angel."

AO1 Dunhill-Cooper grew up in Denver, Colorado, and San Francisco, California. When he was a kid, he loved BMX, sports and Boy Scouts.

MESSAGE FROM A BLUE
AM1 Matthew Bellin

"If you want to be a Blue Angel, go for that! It doesn't matter how early it is. Start aiming towards it now."

AM1 Bellin grew up in Green Bay, Wisconsin.

So, you want to be a Blue Angel?
Here's what you do.

Dream big;
Study hard;
Stay out of trouble;
Don't do drugs;
Learn math and science;
Play team sports;
Graduate high school, and;
Join the Navy or the Marine Corps.
And someday, you could be a Blue Angel too!

More Blue Angels

Visit www.BlueAngelsBook.us for:

Coloring pages
Videos
Facebook
And more!

Naval Aviation Museum

The Naval Aviation Museum is next door to the Florida home of the Blue Angels, on Naval Air Station Pensacola.

The museum is a place where you can see and touch more than 150 aircraft, watch the Blue Angels practice, take a ride in a simulator and much, much more. Admission is free and the museum is open all year. Visit www.BlueAngelsBook.us for more info.

And ask an adult to call your local Science Center or Airplane Museum to see if there are any Blue Angels aircraft in your town.

In the Midwest U.S., a Blue Angel display was opened in 2012 in St. Louis, Missouri, at the St. Louis Science Center.

CPSIA information can be obtained at www.ICGtesting.com
Printed in the USA
BVOW07s1647190815

414023BV00008B/23/P